RACIAL JUSTICE IN AMERICA
ASIAN AMERICAN PACIFIC ISLANDER

What Is YELLOW PERIL?

VIRGINIA LOH-HAGAN

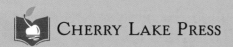

Published in the United States of America by Cherry Lake Publishing Group
Ann Arbor, Michigan
www.cherrylakepublishing.com

Reading Adviser: Beth Walker Gambro, MS, Ed., Reading Consultant, Yorkville, IL
Book Design and Cover Art: Felicia Macheske

Photo Credits: © insta_photos/Shutterstock.com, 5; © Daisy Daisy/Shutterstock.com, 7; © Anonymousz/Shutterstock.com, 9; © Niloo/Shutterstock.com, 11; Library of Congress, Photo by Fred Palumbo, 1964, LOC Control No: 94512334, 12; Library of Congress, Engraving by Thure de Thulstrup, LOC Control No: 89708533, 15; © Jerel Cooper/Shutterstock.com, 16; © Sirisak_baokaew/Shutterstock.com, 19; © MPH Photos/Shutterstock.com, 21; © Yulia.Panova/Shutterstock.com, 22; © Gorodenkoff/Shutterstock.com, 25; © Cavan-Images/Shutterstock.com, 27; © Halfpoint/Shutterstock.com, 29; © Rido/Shutterstock.com, 30

Graphics Throughout: © debra hughes/Shutterstock.com

Library of Congress Cataloging-in-Publication Data

Names: Loh-Hagan, Virginia, author.
Title: What is yellow peril? / by Virginia Loh-Hagan.
Description: Ann Arbor : Cherry Lake Publishing, [2022] | Series: Racial justice in America: Asian American Pacific Islander | Audience: Grades 4-6 | Summary: "Students will learn about yellow peril and discover how it endangers lives and leads to racially motivated hate crimes against Asian American Pacific Islanders (AAPI) in America. This series explores the issues specific to the AAPI community in a comprehensive, honest, and age-appropriate way. Series is written by Virginia Loh-Hagan, a prolific author, advocate, and director of the San Diego State University Asian Pacific Islander Desi American Resource Center. Developed in conjunction with educator, advocate, and author Kelisa Wing, these books were created to reach children of all races and encourage them to approach race issues with open eyes and minds. Books include 21st Century Skills and content, an activity across books, table of contents, glossary, index, author biography, sidebars, and educational matter"—Provided by publisher.
Identifiers: LCCN 2021047052 | ISBN 9781534199385 (hardcover) | ISBN 9781668900529 (paperback) | ISBN 9781668906286 (ebook) | ISBN 9781668901960 (pdf)
Subjects: LCSH: Asian Americans—Social conditions—Juvenile literature. | Pacific Islander Americans—Social conditions—Juvenile literature. | Asian Americans—Crimes against—Juvenile literature. | Hate crimes—United States—Juvenile literature. | Racism—United States—History—Juvenile literature. | Anti-racism—United States--Juvenile literature. | United States—Race relations—Juvenile literature.
Classification: LCC E184.A75 L64 2022 | DDC 305.895/073—dc23
LC record available at https://lccn.loc.gov/2021047052

Cherry Lake Publishing Group would like to acknowledge the work of the Partnership for 21st Century Learning, a Network of Battelle for Kids. Please visit *http://www.battelleforkids.org/networks/p21* for more information.

Printed in the United States of America

Dr. Virginia Loh-Hagan is an author, former K-8 teacher, curriculum designer, and university professor. She's currently the Director of the Asian Pacific Islander Desi American (APIDA) Center at San Diego State University. She identifies as Chinese American and is committed to amplifying APIDA communities. She lives in San Diego with her one very tall husband and two very naughty dogs.

CHAPTER 1

What Is Yellow Peril?

Asian Americans are a strong community. But like other people of color, they are suffering. They are denied justice. They struggle under White **supremacy**.

In the 1960s, activists first used the term "Asian American." They wanted to unite Asian groups. Before this, Asian immigrants were known by their **ethnicities**. For example, they were called "Chinese American" or "Indian American." They acted as separate groups. But they were mistreated as one big group. So they joined forces. As "Asian Americans," they had more power.

Today, they are also called "Asian American Pacific Islander (AAPI)." Another term is "Asian Pacific Islander **Desi** American (APIDA)." These terms are more **inclusive**, meaning that they apply to more Asian people. But they don't fully represent this community.

Asian Americans are diverse. They have unique cultures, histories, and languages. It's important to remember this.

Asian Americans are part of the American story. They have made significant contributions and continue to do so. Yet, they are often pushed to the margins. In the 1800s, they immigrated in large numbers. Since then, they have faced **discrimination**. They have fought to be seen and heard. Their fight for racial justice continues today.

Think about what you have learned in school. How many Asian Americans did you study?

"Yellow Peril" is the name of a racist movement. It is the idea that Asians are dangerous. It is a fear of Asians taking over. It serves as a warning to the Western world. It is rooted in xenophobia. Xenophobia is the fear or dislike of people from other countries. Asians are sometimes seen as foreign invaders or as the enemy. They are seen as a threat to White supremacy.

Yellow Peril is a racist color metaphor. A metaphor is a figure of speech describing something in a non-literal way. Identifying people in terms of skin color is common practice. It simplifies race, which is very complex. But it is important to know people cannot be reduced to a color.

Yellow usually refers to East Asians. East Asians include Chinese, Koreans, and Japanese. But yellow can apply to all people with Asian backgrounds. However, some South and Southeast Asians identify themselves as Brown Asians. Because of the word's connection to Yellow Peril, yellow can be seen as an insult. It should not be used to describe Asians. In some cases, activists have reclaimed the word. They describe the Asian American movement as "yellow power."

This book unpacks Yellow Peril. Learn more so that you can do more. Help fight against White supremacy.

Think about how we use language to describe people. Why are words important?

AMPLIFY AN ACTIVIST!

Activists change our world for the better. Meet Yellow Pearl! Yellow Pearl is a band. The members are Chris Kando Iijima, Nobuko JoAnne Miyamoto, and Charlie Chin. They use music as activism. Their songs are about Asian American power. Chin said, "...we had helped build this country and had a right to be here."

CHAPTER 2

What Is the History of Yellow Peril?

Yellow Peril is based on the fear of rising Asian power. It's the belief that Asian countries are going to take over Europe and the United States. White people feared being invaded and enslaved by Asians.

Fear of Asians dates back to the 13th century. At that time, Mongolia was the largest land empire. Mongol armies invaded many lands across Asia and Europe. They were fierce warriors. Most Europeans had never seen Asians before. There were great differences between the two groups. Their looks, languages, and customs were strange to each other. These differences were used to create fear and distrust.

Yellow Peril is **propaganda**. Propaganda is using **biased** or misleading information to promote an idea. The idea behind Yellow Peril is that Asians are bad and must be excluded or conquered. The main purpose of Yellow Peril is to maintain White supremacy. Like most propaganda, Yellow Peril relies on the media.

Yellow Peril propaganda began with sociologist Jacques Novikov. In 1897, he wrote an essay called "The Yellow Peril." He told people to be suspicious of Asians. He encouraged the use of race as a way to judge people.

Think about how European armies have been invading and raiding for thousands of years. Why are Asian invasions different?

Wilhelm II was a German emperor. He was inspired by Novikov's essay. He used it to encourage European countries to conquer Asia. He had a dream and had it made into a painting. This painting was of an angel leading an army against Asian forces. It was published in an American magazine. It was titled *The Yellow Peril*.

The Yellow Peril idea took hold. William Randolph Hearst was an American publisher. He controlled the largest chain of newspapers. In many of his publications, he promoted Yellow Peril. Many Americans read these stories. They believed the propaganda. They thought Asians were dangerous.

Yellow Peril propaganda was used to support imperialism. In the late 1800s, the United States and other Western powers wanted to expand their territories. They wanted to increase their resources. In order to do this, they had to conquer other lands. The United States conquered lands in the Pacific Islands. To justify their actions, they dehumanized those they conquered. Many articles pictured Asians as animals or children. The images were very offensive. Believing Asians were "other" made it easier to oppress them. This is a common practice done to hurt communities of color.

Think about how many advertisements you see in a day. What ideas are being put into your head?

LEARN FROM OUR PAST!

Let's not repeat the mistakes of our past. In 1898, Guam became a U.S. territory. It is in a strategic location between the Americas and Asia. The U.S. Navy created a dump on Guam. It dumped military waste there. This pollution has caused environmental problems. Treating lands and people like trash hurts everyone.

Yellow Peril propaganda was also used to keep Asians out of the United States. Asian workers came to the United States in the 1800s. They helped build the Transcontinental Railroad. They worked on farms and opened businesses. They worked for less money than White workers. Many White workers lost their jobs. They blamed Chinese workers. They demanded the United States ban Asian immigration.

Think about all the rights you have. What rights were denied to people of color?

Denis Kearney was a California labor leader. He said, "The Chinese must go!" This became a popular slogan for the Yellow Peril movement. Several racist laws were passed to exclude Asians. The Page Act of 1875 banned Chinese women from immigrating. The Chinese Exclusion Act of 1882 banned Chinese workers from immigrating. The Geary Act of 1892 extended these bans. The Immigration Act of 1917 created Asian Barred Zones. This banned immigrants from Asian countries.

Yellow Peril was used to justify Japanese incarceration. In 1941, Japan attacked Pearl Harbor in Hawaii. This caused the United States to enter World War II (1939–1945). Many people were afraid that Japanese Americans would be loyal to Japan instead of the United States. President Franklin D. Roosevelt issued an order forcing Japanese Americans into internment camps.

White Americans feared Asians would destroy racial purity. Asian immigrants were banned from marrying outside of their race. They were denied many rights.

CHAPTER 3

What Does Yellow Peril Look Like Today?

Racist laws were the result of Yellow Peril. Today many of these laws have been overturned. But they have caused lingering damage. Throughout history, Asian Americans have been the victims of many hate crimes.

The Chinese Massacre of 1871 took place in Los Angeles, California. Chinese gangs fought. A White citizen was killed. Word spread that the Chinese "were killing Whites." A mob of 500 White Americans raided Chinatown. They hanged 19 Chinese immigrants.

On September 2, 1885, another massacre took place. It was in Rock Springs, Wyoming. Coal mine companies hired Chinese workers. A mob of White workers set fire to about 80 Chinese homes. About 30 Chinese people died, and about 15 were injured. Others fled.

On September 7, 1885, Chinese workers were attacked in Squak Valley, Washington. A White mob fired guns into tents where Chinese workers slept. Three Chinese men died. Three were hurt.

On November 3, 1885, White city leaders marched Chinese immigrants to a train station in Tacoma, Washington. In 1886, a White mob in Seattle raided homes. They forced more than 300 Chinese immigrants on ships and trains.

In 1887, the Snake River Massacre occurred in Oregon. More than 30 Chinese miners were robbed and killed.

Think about the immigration history of Asian Americans. Why were there more hate crimes against Chinese immigrants in the 1800s?

Think about the definition of hate crimes. How are hate crimes different from other crimes?

STAY ACTIVE ON SOCIAL!

Stay connected on social media. It is a great way to learn more. Follow these hashtags:

- **#StopAsianHate** This hashtag was created because of the anti-Asian hate related to COVID-19. It supports the Stop Asian Hate movement.

- **#StopAAPIHate** This hashtag represents an organization collecting and sharing data about anti-Asian hate.

In the 1970s, Vietnamese refugees settled in the United States. They were escaping from war and poverty in Vietnam. A group settled in Seadrift, Texas. They became shrimp fishermen. This upset many White fishermen. White mobs formed. They set boats on fire. In 1979, a fight broke out between Vietnamese and White fishermen. A White man was killed. The Ku Klux Klan is a White supremacy group. They helped the White mobs. They hosted rallies against the Vietnamese refugees. They followed the refugees in the water and threatened to shoot them.

In 1982, Vincent Chin was a Chinese American living in Detroit, Michigan. Two White men had lost their jobs at a Detroit car factory. They blamed the Japanese auto industry. The men assumed Chin was Japanese and killed him at a bar. One of them was heard saying, "It's because of you . . . that we're out of work."

In 1989, a White gunman shot at an elementary school in Stockton, California. He talked openly about hating Asian immigrants. He blamed them for taking away jobs from White workers. He killed five children. More than 30 were wounded. Most of the victims were Southeast Asian refugees.

On September 11, 2001, terrorists attacked the United States. South Asian Americans became "the other." They were blamed for the attacks. Many were bullied.

In December 2019, the COVID-19 pandemic broke out. The first case was in China. Then it spread worldwide. People feared becoming sick. This set the stage for race-based hate caused by Yellow Peril. Asian Americans are often seen as perpetual or forever foreigners. They're seen as outsiders.

President Donald Trump called COVID-19 the "Kung Flu" and the "China Virus." Such comments helped spread Yellow Peril. Hate crimes against those with Asian backgrounds increased by 150 percent in 2020. Some people blamed the virus on anyone with an Asian background. Asian Americans were called racist names. They were harassed and attacked. Many elderly Asian Americans were targeted. On March 16, 2021, a gunman killed six Asian American women at a spa in Atlanta, Georgia.

Racism has made it harder for Asian Americans to make a living. Businesses owned by Asian Americans have suffered. Chinatown communities have collapsed.

Yellow Peril has kept customers away. Some people think these places are centers for the disease. This is far from true. Research shows that there are fewer COVID-19 cases in Chinatowns than in other neighborhoods. People can't catch a disease from an ethnicity.

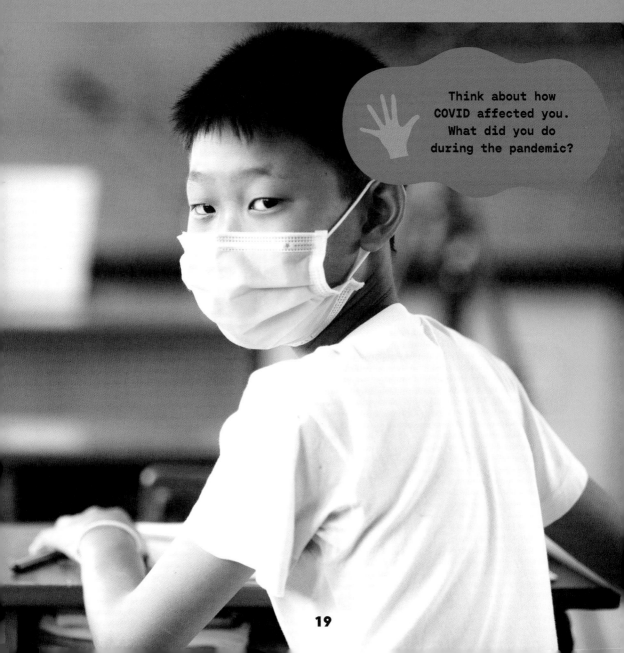

Think about how COVID affected you. What did you do during the pandemic?

CHAPTER 4

Why Is Yellow Peril Problematic?

Hate crimes are the worst result of Yellow Peril. But it had other effects. Some people formed hate groups. They organized against Asian immigrants. Forming groups that oppress people is dangerous. It hurts a lot of people. It stops us from being a free society.

In 1876, the Los Angeles Anti-Coolie Club was formed. *Coolie* is a racist word used to describe Chinese workers. The club's goal was to "protect the White people residing in America from Chinese labor . . . ."

In the 1880s, the Anti-Chinese League formed in Tombstone, Arizona. Its members agreed to not hire any Chinese workers. They boycotted Chinese businesses and started riots.

In 1905, White labor leaders in San Francisco formed the Japanese and Korean Exclusion League. In 1907, they became the Asiatic Exclusion League. They fought to ban Asian immigration.

In 1908, the Anti-Jap Laundry League started in San Francisco. Its members wanted to put Japanese-owned laundries out of business. They picketed outside of their stores. They followed customers home and bullied them. They prevented businesses from selling equipment to Japanese Americans. They threatened city leaders.

Think about the groups you belong to. Do you help or hurt others?

Think about a hard time
in your life. Who or
what do you blame?

When things go wrong, people look for a reason. Yellow Peril made it easy to blame Asian immigrants. To White Americans, everything about the Asians was strange. They looked and acted differently. This made them an easy target. Asian immigrants became America's scapegoats. They were blamed for national security and economic issues. They were blamed for public health crises.

Yellow Peril said that Asians were dangerous and dirty. It relied on offensive stereotypes, which are widely held beliefs about a group of people. Asian immigrants were often pictured with buck teeth and squinty eyes. They were assumed to be spies. They were accused of plotting to take away property and jobs from White people. They were believed to carry diseases. They were seen as criminals.

In 1877, the California Senate published a formal report. The report said Chinese immigrants had destroyed American values. It blamed Chinese immigrants for increased crime. It stated, ". . .a hundred White have been contaminated by their presence."

Asian immigrants were also seen as inferior. Denis Kearney said that White Americans should not have to "compete with the single Chinese coolie. . . . To an American, death is preferable to life on a par with the Chinaman."

Yellow Peril stereotypes exist today. The media continues to play a huge role in promoting these stereotypes in books, movies, and TV shows. Asian Americans need better representation. They need to be featured more. They need to be pictured in more positive, accurate ways.

Several stereotypes exist about Asian men. In some images, Asian men are seen as evil criminals. They are portrayed as sly and tricky. They are thought to prey on White women. In other images, they are emasculated. They are portrayed as weak. This makes them less attractive and less threatening.

Asian women also fight against stereotypes. These stereotypes have names such as Dragon Lady and Lotus Blossom. They are accused of seducing White men. They are valued only for how they serve others.

None of these stereotypes are true. Believing these stereotypes is dangerous. First, it is wrong to clump people together and assume things apply to all of them. Second, it is wrong to use race as a reason to hate. Today, more than ever, we need to celebrate Asian Americans. Sandra Oh is an actress. She said, "It's an honor just to be Asian."

Think about the last movie you saw. Were Asian Americans in it? If so, how were they depicted?

BE IN THE KNOW!

Other concepts to know:

- **Eurocentrism** This is the idea that Whiteness is the desired standard. It centers on European people and cultures. It's seeing the world in terms of White values and experiences.

- **Othering** This is a process of placing a group of people outside the norm. It assumes this group is a threat.

CHAPTER 5

How Can We Be Better?

You have learned about the problems with Yellow Peril. Let's work to stop it.

We all come from different positions and types of **privilege**. Privilege is a special right or advantage. It is given to a chosen person or group. It is not earned. In the United States, being White is a privilege. Other examples include being male or an English speaker. It's hard to get ahead in a world that is not made for you. Use your privileges. Help oppressed people achieve equality.

Start with Yourself!

Everybody can do something. Just start somewhere. Start small. Build your self-awareness and your knowledge.

- Learn more about the history of anti-Asian hate in America. Hate crimes and incidents against Asian Americans aren't new. They have been happening since Asians immigrated to the United States.

- Learn more about the current wave of anti-Asian hate. Watch the news. Read articles. Keep up on social media.

- Unlearn the stereotypes of Asian Americans and other people of color. Judge people as individuals.

- Unlearn messages you hear in the media. Question assumptions. Be critical. Challenge racist thinking. Don't believe propaganda.

Think about your privileges. What powers and resources do you have?

Be an Ally!

Being an ally is the first step in racial justice work. Allies recognize their privilege. They use it in solidarity with others. They see something and they say something.

- Speak to your Asian American friends. Let them know you are aware of the current wave of anti-Asian hate. Ask them about their experiences. Ask them about their feelings. Check in on them. Make sure they are okay.

- Speak up when people say something about Asians taking over. Tell them they need to do more research. Offer to learn more together.

- Speak up when people say, "All Asians look alike." Tell them this is a racist comment.

- Speak up when people assume Asian Americans are not from here. Explain there is a difference between Asians and Asian Americans. Tell them to be less xenophobic.

Be an Accomplice!

Being an **accomplice** goes beyond allyship. Accomplices use their privilege. They challenge supremacy. They are willing to be uncomfortable. They stand up for equal rights.

- Stand with Asian Americans. Support Asian-owned businesses and Asian American artists. Support Asian American politicians. Encourage others to do the same.

- Stand united against anti-Asian hate. Participate in peaceful protests. Be safe. Make sure an adult is with you.

Think about your powers and resources. How would your life be different without them?

Be an Activist!

Activists actively fight for political or social change. They give up their own privileges. They work together to fight racism. They understand that if one group suffers, all groups suffer.

- Fight for more Asian American representation in popular culture. Seeing Asian Americans in the media makes them seem less foreign. Write letters to film and TV companies. Post requests on social media.

- Fight for more Asian American representation in your school. Give up your leadership roles for others to have a voice.

- Fight for Black Lives Matter. Fight against negative stereotypes of people of color. Yellow Peril exists because anti-Blackness exists.

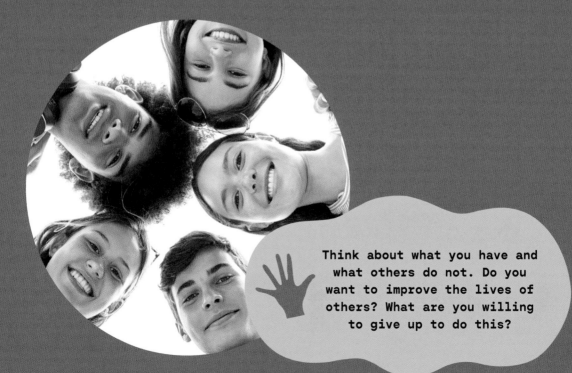

Think about what you have and what others do not. Do you want to improve the lives of others? What are you willing to give up to do this?

Take the Challenge!

Read all the books in the "Racial Justice in America" series. Engage in the community of activism. Create a podcast, newsletter, video, or social media campaign. Show up for the Asian American community. Include a segment about Yellow Peril.

TASK: Compare and contrast anti-Asian hate in the past and anti-Asian hate today. Read oral histories. Conduct interviews. Study the reports on the Stop AAPI Hate website: https://stopaapihate.org/reportincident/.

Share your learning. Encourage others to learn more. Then, when you know more, do more. Commit to racial justice!

WHAT WOULD YOU DO?

Imagine you're meeting friends for lunch. One of your friends says, "I don't want Asian food. All Asians eat dogs." How does this comment promote Yellow Peril? What would you do?

☐ Laugh.

☐ Ignore it.

☐ Change the subject.

☐ Say something.

EXTEND YOUR LEARNING

FICTION

James, Helen Foster, and Virginia Shin-Mui Loh. *Paper Son: Lee's Journey to America*. Ann Arbor, MI: Sleeping Bear Press, 2013.

Yin. *Coolies*. New York, NY: Philomel Books, 2001.

NONFICTION

Brockenborough, Martha. *I Am an American: The Wong Kim Ark Story*. New York, NY: Little, Brown and Company, 2021.

Loh-Hagan, Virginia. *A is for Asian American: An Asian Pacific Islander Desi American Alphabet Book*. Ann Arbor, MI: Sleeping Bear Press, 2022.

Takaki, Ronald. *A Different Mirror for Young People: A History of Multicultural America*. New York, NY: Seven Stories Press, 2012.

Public Broadcasting Service: Asian Americans
www.pbs.org/weta/asian-americans/

GLOSSARY

accomplice (uh-KAHM-pluhss) a person who uses their privilege to fight against supremacy

ally (AH-lye) a person who is aware of their privilege and supports oppressed communities

biased (BYE-uhst) misleading or showing preference for a particular perspective or person

coolie (KOO-lee) a racist word used to describe a Chinese or Asian worker

dehumanized (dee-HYOO-muh-nyzd) deprived of human qualities and made inferior

Desi (DEH-see) a word that describes people from India, Pakistan, or Bangladesh

discrimination (dih-skrih-muh-NAY-shuhn) the unjust or unfair treatment of different categories of people

emasculated (ih-MAH-skyuh-layt-uhd) having deprived a man of his male role or identity; to make weaker or less effective

ethnicities (eth-NIH-suh-teez) the states of belonging to a social group that has a common national or cultural tradition

imperialism (ihm-PIHR-ee-uh-liz-uhm) a policy of extending a country's power and influence through diplomacy or military force

inclusive (ihn-KLOO-siv) allowing all kinds of people to belong

massacre (MAH-sih-kuhr) a brutal slaughter of a group of people

metaphor (MEH-tuh-for) a figure of speech that describes an object or action in a way that isn't literally true but that helps explain an idea or make a comparison

peril (PEHR-uhl) danger

perpetual (puhr-PEH-chuh-wuhl) forever, never-ending

propaganda (prah-puh-GAN-duh) biased information used to promote a particular political cause or point of view

privilege (PRIV-lij) a unearned right or advantage given to a chosen person or group

refugees (reh fyoo-JEEZ) people who have been forced to leave their country in order to escape war, persecution, or natural disaster

scapegoats (SKAYP-gohtss) people or groups being blamed for wrongdoings, mistakes, or faults of others

stereotypes (STEHR-ee-uh-typss) widely held ideas or beliefs many people have about a thing or group, which may be untrue or only partly true

supremacy (suh-PREH-muh-see) the idea that one group is superior to other groups and thus is given privileges to maintain that power

xenophobia (zeh-nuh-FOH-bee-uh) the fear or dislike of people from other countries

INDEX